Remembering
Johnny

Remembering
Johnny

The King of Late Night
Looking Back

On Sunday, January 23, 2005, Americans reeled from the news that Johnny Carson, the man who had tucked them in for thirty years as beloved host of *The Tonight Show*, had succumbed to the effects of emphesyma at the age of seventy-nine. Yes, the reserved icon had kept quiet about his illness, but it was something more. Interviewing Johnny's longtime sidekick Ed McMahon on the *Today* show, Katie Couric summed it up: "Johnny Carson seemed kind of immortal."

As tributes poured in from show-business superstars and people in the street, the magnitude of Johnny Carson's impact on this country became clear. President George W. Bush saluted him as "a steady and reassuring presence in homes across America for three decades," adding "his wit and insight made Americans laugh and think and had a profound influence on American life and entertainment."

Here's a look back at how a Midwestern boy with a big dream and a bigger spirit became television's biggest star.

Growing Up Carson

Johnny and his brother Dick loved to vanish into the woods for fishing expeditions. "I could have paved a highway with all the peanut butter sandwiches I made for them," said their mother Ruth.

"I was so naive as a kid I used to sneak behind the barn and do nothing."

Johnny Carson

John William Carson was born October 23, 1925, in Corning, Iowa, the middle child of Homer L. ("Kit") Carson, a manager for Iowa and Nebraska Light and Power, and Ruth Hook Carson, an outgoing homemaker. When Johnny was barely eight, the family moved to a modest two-story house in Norfolk, Nebraska, where Johnny enjoyed a fairly ordinary childhood. A decent student, he discovered early on that he could attract attention by telling stories.

Johnny's babysitter reads to him and his younger brother, Dick (right), who would grow up to be a *Tonight Show* director.

One of Carson's first animal guests.

The Great Carsoni's professional debut came at the age of fourteen, when he performed for the Norfolk Rotary Club for a whopping $3.

Carson was also intrigued by comedy, and he showed an aptitude for it early on. On Sundays he'd station himself next to the family radio and memorize the routines of his comedy idol, Jack Benny, then try them out at school the next week. He also honed his own comedy writing in a humor column for his high school newspaper. Johnny's close friend Larry Sanford was right on the money with his inspiration in Johnny's 1943 yearbook: "John, if you don't get killed in the war you'll be a hell of an entertainer some day."

THE GREAT CARSONI

When he was twelve years old, Johnny stumbled upon *Professor Hoffmann's Book of Magic* and was smitten. He immediately sent away for a mail-order magic kit and threw himself into mastering card tricks and other sleights of hand. Fascinated by the exploits of master magician and escape artist Harry Houdini, he called himself "the Great Carsoni," and for his thirteenth birthday received from his theatrically-minded mother a magician's worktable that he draped with a black cloth embroidered with his new stage name. A life in show business had begun.

Johnny enlisted in the U.S. Navy right after graduation. Commissioned as an ensign during World War II's final days, Johnny was on his way to his assignment in the Pacific aboard the battleship U.S.S. *Pennsylvania* when the atomic bombs fell on Hiroshima and Nagasaki. He reported for duty on the last day of the war, August 14, 1945.

Johnny received a warm welcome at the school where he had once locked a cow in a third-floor chemistry lab overnight. During his 1981 graduation address, he joked "I could have also been the most famous graduate of Norfolk High if I had gone to the electric chair.

After the war, Carson enrolled at the University of Nebraska, where he could be found in student theater productions like *She Was Only a Pharaoh's Daughter but She Never Became a Mummy*, in which he played Cleopatra. While earning his bachelor's degree—in just three years—he held down a part-time job at Lincoln, Nebraska's radio station KFAB, where he created a comedic western. The university let him make comedy writing his senior thesis; the final product was a recording of the era's funnymen doing their acts, accompanied by Johnny's audio commentary explaining why the routines worked.

After his 1949 graduation, Carson landed a job hosting the afternoon interview program *The Squirrel's Nest* for radio station WOW in Omaha. At that time, local radio stations received prewritten questions along with prerecorded answers from celebrities; all Johnny had to do was read the text and play the reply. But he wasn't above having a little fun with the format. On one occasion, instead of asking Patti Page when she started singing, he said, "I understand you're hitting the bottle pretty good, Patti . . . when did you start?" Her recorded answer, "When I was 6 I used to get up at church socials and do it," took on a whole new meaning.

Mal Hansen, who was then farm director at the station, said he remembered Carson as a hardworking and talented announcer. "The audience in Omaha loved him," Hansen told *USA Today*. "At the same time, he was rather modest. He was not one of these showoff guys you sometimes run into in that profession."

Johnny maintained that blend of confidence and modesty throughout his career—just one of the reasons President Bush said that Carson "always remembered his roots in the heartland." Johnny himself, in an NBC special that followed him to his hometown, remembered his Midwestern youth as "an era that gave you direction in life." Pretty soon, that direction pointed west—to Los Angeles.

TV Before
Tonight

As television replaced radio as the focal point of American living rooms, Carson made the transition too. He had whetted his appetite with a virtually unwatched experimental broadcast while at the University of Nebraska, and now he was ready to plunge into the young industry that, at first, didn't know what to make of him.

The US Steel Hour variety show was just one of the many programs to which Johnny lent his talents during the years prior to *The Tonight Show*.

Johnny Carson as a television up-and-comer.

CARSON'S CELLAR

After his 1950 move to Los Angeles, Carson talked the powers that be at KNXT-TV into giving him a Sunday afternoon sketch comedy show, *Carson's Cellar*. It was a low-budget operation with few viewers, but, as it turned out, there was one very important one.

One afternoon, when a figure scurried across the set, Johnny joked that it was comedy luminary Red Skelton and that they simply didn't have time to put him on the show. Skelton happened to be tuning in and loving the show. He unexpectedly turned up the next week at *Carson's Cellar*, demanding to make an appearance.

Word spread about this gem of a show and soon the likes of Groucho Marx and Johnny's boyhood idol Jack Benny were making unpaid visits. When *Carson's Cellar* folded in 1953, Skelton snapped Carson up to write on his CBS program.

Interviewing Carson in 1992 for *60 Minutes*, Mike Wallace quoted *Johnny Carson Show* producer Ben Brady: "He is genetically not a strong stand-up comedian like Hope, Skelton, or Benny. He isn't now, and he never can be." Replied Johnny, "well, I wonder what Mr. Brady would say today."

Indignities such as the costume for this *Johnny Carson Show* food commercial must have had Johnny contemplating a return to radio.

Even flanked by "Carson's Cuties" Johnny didn't attract enough viewers
to keep *The Johnny Carson Show* afloat.

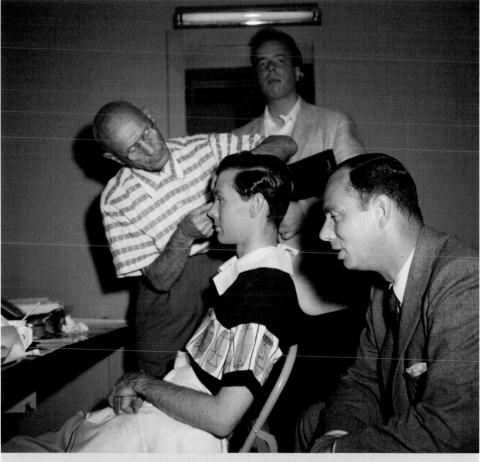

Johnny getting dolled up for the low-budget *Carson's Cellar* in 1952.

Johnny behind the spotlight at
The Johnny Carson Show in 1956.

A skilled jazz drummer, Johnny loved to jump behind the
kit with *The Johnny Carson Show* band.

When Ed McMahon auditioned for the job as Johnny's
announcer for *Who Do You Trust?* in 1958, he doubted that
he'd won the job because Johnny was so aloof. "I learned
later he made up his mind the minute he shook hands
with me," said McMahon.

THE JOHNNY CARSON SHOW ...
AFTER SHOW, AFTER SHOW

Not long into his tenure on Red Skelton's show, Johnny got
a fortunate break, which followed Mr. Skelton's unfortu-
nate one: he'd knocked himself out doing a stunt just two
hours before show time. Panicked producers had no choice
but to let Johnny go on in Skelton's place. Johnny rose to
the occasion and opened with a monologue he'd written
while driving to the studio. Jack Benny saw him in action
and said "The kid is great, just great ... You better watch
that Carson kid!"

Thrilled with his performance, the network tried
Carson out on a number of shows, but nothing seemed to
click. The game show *Earn Your Vacation* came and went
in a year, and the variety show *The Johnny Carson Show* last-
ed just thirty-nine weeks. Seven writers and eight directors
passed through its revolving door without unlocking the
talent that Johnny obviously had in abundance.

WHO DO YOU TRUST?

The months after *The Johnny Carson Show* folded found Johnny in New York doing appearances on several shows, including *The Tonight Show* under host Jack Paar. In 1957, the ABC network took him on as host of the game show *Who Do You Trust?,* which featured an announcer with a booming voice named Ed McMahon. Perhaps because of its format, which allowed a lot of back-and-forth between host and guests, Carson finally had a hit on his hands and the show ran five years. But greater things lay just around the corner.

A promo shot for *Who Do You Trust?*

'62-'63

'63-'64

'65-'66

'64-'65

'66-'67

'67-'68

'68-'69

'69-'70

'70-'71

'71-'72

'2-'73

'73-'74

'74-'75

'7

'77-'78

'78-'79

'79-'

'81-'82

The Many Faces of Johnny: Johnny presents . . .
himself, twenty of them during an anniversary special.

The Tonight Show Years:
1962–1992

Johnny with his fellow television innovator, Groucho Marx,
who hosted *You Bet Your Life.*

When Jack Paar decided he'd had enough after five years as the host of *The Tonight Show,* NBC asked the up-and-coming Johnny Carson to replace him. After a six-month delay caused by ABC's refusal to release him from his *Who Do You Trust?* contract, Johnny stepped into the job on October 1, 1962.

Groucho Marx introduced him, and as an ovation greeted Johnny's first appearance on the stage, he looked surprised. "Boy, you would think it was Vice President Nixon!" he exclaimed.

Someone once asked Johnny Carson
what he would like his epitaph to be.
He thought for a moment, smiled, and said,

"I'll be right back."

"Johnny hosted the show for thirty years. Think about that. These days some NBC shows don't last thirty days."

Jay Leno

ABOVE
Like Johnny, Steve Allen, *The Tonight Show*'s first host, was notorious for not speaking to his guests during commercial breaks. Steve Allen hosted from 1954–1957.

BELOW
Nobody would have predicted that Carson would last for thirty years after the innovative and mercurial Jack Paar burned out in just five years.

At its height of its popularity, *The Tonight Show* drew 15 million viewers nightly, and was responsible for 17 percent of the network's profit. It was the most financially successful show in television history.

Paul Anka's theme song—*daa dat dat da da*—became "America's lullaby." Over the years, Johnny's writers included comedy heavyweights such as Dick Cavett and Woody Allen.

Johnny was enraged when an unidentified NBC technician taped over hundreds of hours of early episodes in a cost-saving measure. This inspired him to push for tighter control culminating in ownership of his *Tonight Show* material.

NEW YORK AND THE MOVE TO CALIFORNIA: GRAVITY SHIFTS

New York City in the 1960s was on an upswing: The Mets and the Jets were on top of the world, the city was the home to the World's Fair and its mayor, the charismatic John Lindsay was poised for a presidential race. Only a kid from the Midwest could come to New York, master its coolness, sophistication and edge and reintroduce it to the rest of America not in a form they merely accepted, but in one they ate up. Perhaps this was because Carson always loved to rib the town he jokingly called "Fun City" about the very things that separated it from the rest of America and its apple-pie charm.

Average Americans trusted Johnny, even in his Nehru jacket, cocktail-party days, because they always understood that he was one of them: the kid who left the farm and made good in the big city. As Dick Cavett recalled in the *New York Times*, "I'm sure he was a little uncomfortable in New York, in the way ordinary people from the Midwest are about making a faux pas, like a guy with some straw still stuck to his shoes."

Though Carson had become a star in the New York firmament, he knew his show was about the guests, and there were more movie stars in LA than in New York. Fittingly, only a month after his fellow Midwesterners in the Wisconsin primary rejected the man Johnny had put on the national stage, John Lindsay, he packed his bags and moved to Los Angeles.

> ## "Any time four New Yorkers get into a cab together without arguing, a bank robbery has just taken place."
>
> *Johnny Carson*

> ## "It was a migration that . . . essentially marked the end of Manhattan's parity with Hollywood as a glitz capital for a national audience."
>
> *Frank Rich, in the* New York Times

Johnny and New York mayor, John Lindsay were both ambitious toasts of the town but only Johnny's appeal worked west of the Hudson.

"He was our little bad boy," said frequent guest Dr. Joyce Brothers, "but never so so bad that we'd be embarrassed by him."

NETWORK BATTLES

There were bumps in the road. In 1967, Carson walked out over a salary dispute and stayed away for weeks until the network gave him a contract reportedly worth over $1 million a year.

Years later, in 1979, when NBC president Fred Silverman, looking for ways to increase ratings, complained about Johnny's vacation time, Johnny fired back with an announcement that he'd quit after his contract expired. NBC panicked and gave him what was at that time the most lucrative contract in television history: a $5 million salary plus commitments to his production company, Carson Productions, for several other shows, including *TV's Bloopers and Practical Jokes*. Overall, the deal was worth more than $50 million, an unimaginable sum in those days. Also at this time Johnny won ownership of the shows and therefore any profits from future sales, like classic collections on videotape. Asked at the time if his deal meant that NBC was in trouble, Johnny said "That's like saying the Titanic had a small leak."

Even into his final years, Johnny kept sticking it to the suits upstairs. At the end of 1991, he told his audience that General Electric's Christmas card read "in lieu of a gift, a G.E. employee has been laid off in your name."

There were ups and downs during Johnny's thirty years at *The Tonight Show*'s helm. The show's demise was predicted time and again as new competitors took him on: Joey Bishop, Merv Griffin, Dick Cavett, Joan Rivers, Arsenio Hall, Jon Stewart, and Pat Sajak, among others. Johnny came roaring back to beat every one of them.

Jay Leno explained Johnny's resiliency. "He was hip, but he was smart enough not to be so hip that next year he was out of style."

Johnny also stayed focused. Except for the occasional Las Vegas gig, and a few Academy Award–hosting jobs, he shunned appearances outside of *The Tonight Show*. For his sustained excellence, Johnny was awarded six Emmy awards.

"His show was the American gathering place every night at 11:30 in a way that I can't possibly explain to my teenage children."

— *NBC's Brian Williams*

Dana Carvey, embodying Johnny in 1992, knew that Carson's reaction shots were his stock in trade.

SECRETS TO HIS SUCCESS

"He was everything to everybody," longtime executive producer and close friend Peter Lassally told the *New York Times*, "He was your husband or your neighbor, your son or your friend."

In the words of the *Washington Post*'s Tom Shales, Carson was "a man who was like a next-door neighbor to 20 million people, dropping by to end the day with a few laughs, even when there seemed so little in the world to laugh about."

Viewers got to know Johnny's idiosyncrasies, such as the nervous drumming on the desk, with a cigarette in the early days, with a pen after national attitudes toward tobacco changed. A straightening of his tie was a gesture suitable for any occasion. There were also the reaction shots: a pained grimace at a guest's lapse in taste, or a look of good-natured bewilderment at the parade of peculiarity on his sofa. No wonder Dana Carvey, in his popular impression, leaned on a single phrase: "Weird, wild stuff."

Often Johnny Carson was at his best when things were worst. "He was the master of the save," said frequent guest Carl Reiner in the *New York Times*. "When a joke would bomb, you wouldn't worry because you'd know he'd just make seven jokes out of it." Carson would mock himself for making a lousy joke, grab the overhead microphone and announce, "Attention Kmart shoppers" or, if things were desperate, dance a soft-shoe as Doc Severinsen led the band in "Tea for Two."

> "On the good nights, he was the second best thing you could do in bed—but on his best nights, he was the best."
>
> *Jack Boulware, salon.com*

One night the jokes fell so flat that Johnny set his pages afire and ceremoniously pitched them into a trash can while Doc played *Taps*.

Asked how he became a star, Carson replied "I started in a gaseous state and then I cooled."

"My success just evolved from working hard at the business at hand each day.

Johnny Carson

Johnny's Monologues:
America's Lullaby

Carson's golf swing was the move
with which he dependably sank the
monologues' final punchline.

With his facial expressions, Johnny let ordinary Americans know that he shared their amazement at Hollywood's and Washington's unusual mores.

"If it weren't for Philo T. Farnsworth, inventor of television, we'd still be eating frozen radio dinners.

Johnny Carson

The jewel in the King of Late Night's crown was the nightly monologue. Everyone was fair game—including himself. Johnny endeared himself to viewers by including his own miseries among the sixteen to twenty-two jokes that opened every show. His failed marriages, the expensive settlements; noisy Con Ed workers disrupting his sleep; his susceptibility to the whims of NBC honchos— Johnny seemingly had nothing to hide.

Carson's one-liners were considered bellwethers for the national mood. When the Watergate-bedeviled Richard Nixon found himself in Johnny's crosshairs, viewers and politicos alike knew the president was through.

Johnny even milked laughs from momentous historical events. After Communism's fall, he told Eastern Europe's citizens what to expect:

"Democracy does not mean having just one ineffective political party; it means having two ineffective political parties . . .

"Democracy is welcoming people from other lands, and giving them something to hold onto—usually a mop or a leaf blower."

After the last joke's delivery came the signature golf swing, and then Johnny would go to the desk, the night's best work often behind him.

His Greatest Episodes

A FEW OF THE INDELIBLE EPISODES FROM TONIGHT SHOW HISTORY INCLUDE:

• Animal guests held a special place in Johnny's heart, and sometimes on his head. Millions watched Joan Embery's skittish marmoset mark its territory.

• The audience gasped when Johnny pretended to snack on Myrtle Young's prize potato chip collection in 1987.

• When a cigar-smoking streaker ran across the set, but wasn't later proscecuted, Johnny quipped to his audience that the culprit had been dismissed for "lack of evidence."

• In an infamous 1963 episode, actor Ed Ames accidentally buried a tomahawk in the nether regions of a cut out sheriff. As the audience roared, Carson cracked "I didn't even know you were Jewish."

Carson didn't tell NBC beforehand when he planned one of his most exhilarating stunts: freefalling 10,000 feet before pulling his parachute's ripcord.

One of the few times Johnny managed to maintain some distance between himself and the visiting wildlife.

Tiny Tim's marriage to Victoria (Miss Vicki) Budinger on Dec 17, 1969, attracted an audience of 45 million—at that time *The Tonight Show*'s biggest ever.

Johnny lived many Americans' dreams when he took the field with Mantle and Maris.

The episode in which Jimmy Stewart's eyes filled while reading a poem about his dog Bo drew some of *The Tonight Show*'s warmest viewer responses.

His Greatest Characters

Carson with his alter egos.

"May a love-starved fruit-fly molest
your sister's nectarines"

Carnac the Magnificent

CARNAC THE MAGNIFICENT
Perhaps the most popular—and recognizable—character in the Carson gallery was
the massively-turbaned seer Carnac the Magnificent.

"May you get your first French
kiss from a diseased camel."

Carnac the Magnificent

ART FERN
"Hello there, feature film freaks."
This sleazy TV pitchman hosted the "Tea Time Movie" alongside his winsome
"Matinee Lady." Art's films included *Abbot and Costello Visit a Leper Colony*
and *Dracula Gets Bombed on a Wino*.

"What's all this fuss about plutonium:How can something named after a Disney character be dangerous?"

Floyd R. Turbo

FLOYD R. TURBO
Dressed in nervous super-patriot Floyd R. Turbo's plaid hunting jacket,
"everyman" Carson wasn't above having a little fun at the everyman's expense.
"He's the epitome of the redneck ignoramus," Johnny once told *Rolling Stone*.

"I only kill in self-defense. What would you do if a rabbit pulled a knife on you?"

Floyd R. Turbo

Johnny bulked up for this homage to Sylvester Stallone's Rambo.

"If life was fair, Elvis would be alive and all the impersonators would be dead."

Johnny Carson

Carson's political leanings remained a closely guarded secret throughout his career. Both the left and the right were targets of his sharp tongue.

Sketch Comedy
Carson Style

Liz Taylor or King Tut?

"He never made you look bad. He wasn't like 'Can you top this?' He always had fun with you and made you feel like you were the guy he wanted to be a hit," said funnyman Don Rickles of his good friend.

Classic horror icons were played for laughs in Carson's signature sketches.

Johnny played Tattoo in a *Fantasy Island* parody.

The Best Guests
Don't Know When to Leave!

Luminaries, politicians, celebrities, rockstars, and ordinary people—everyone loved sitting across from Johnny's desk.

Don Rickles once congratulated McMahon with sincerity upon his recent marriage, then turned to Johnny and barked, "I give it about a week, tops."

Drew Carey was stunned when Carson called him over to his desk to offer his congratulations after Carey's first standup appearance. "That was the greatest day of my whole life," Carey told Leno.

Jackie Mason commented, "He made more stars on his show, probably, than anybody in the whole history of show business."

Even the king of late night got down on his knees before Hollywood royalty Bette Davis.

Johnny gets a flying lesson from Superman Christopher Reeve.

"Pure gold" is how Robin Williams described Carson's unrestrained belly laugh.
"Being on *The Tonight Show* with him was like playing center court at Wimbledon.
Total excitement, and you had to be at the top of your game."

Carson's support gave young Steve Martin a lift, and years later Martin lifted an ailing Johnny's spirits with an invitation to write for the *New Yorker*.

"It wasn't part of your career; it actually was your career," said **Robert Klein**, who was twenty-six—and not yet a star—when he made his first appearance on *The Tonight Show* on January 19, 1968, a date Klein would never forget. "He could not have been more generous to young comedians, but he was also very protective. A lot of the stuff I was doing was pretty hip for the crowds, but he'd really laugh you up and encourage them to laugh, too," Klein told the *New York Times*.

"He had this genuine enjoyment of other people, and especially comedians—that's what you saw on TV," **Ray Romano** said on CNN. "As a comic it was the pinnacle to get on his show and to have him see you perform and to get his validation."

"He could tell when you'd hit comic gold," **Mel Brooks** has said, "and he'd help you mine it."

"His impact cannot be overestimated," said frequent guest host **David Brenner**. "When I walked on stage, I had $3 in my pants pocket. By the close of business the next day, I had $10,000 worth of job offers," recalled Brenner of his first appearance on the show.

"Johnny, you were host to writers, children, intellectuals, and nitwits, and served them all well."

Steve Martin in his New York Times *eulogy*

Ellen DeGeneres was the first female comic to be called over to chat with Carson after she performed, a special honor. Said DeGeneres recently, "he was and will remain the greatest talk-show host we've ever had."

Bette Midler gushed, "Johnny Carson was the public face of American comedy for decades but anyone who knew him well, knew he was an intensely private and yet deeply generous man. So many of us who are working in show business today owe our careers to him.

"He was the greatest talk show host of our time with the quickest mind. To me, he always knew exactly who he was and was always in control. He was a true giant. One of the greatest thrills of my career was not onstage but when Johnny called me after seeing me host the Oscars and telling me how much he loved what I did. That's how much I looked up to him. He was a true idol," reflected **Billy Crystal**.

Heavyweight Champion of the World, Muhammad Ali, encounters the Late-night Champion of the World.

"Johnny was responsible for the beginning and the rise of success for more performers than anyone." said sometime guest host Bill Cosby.

Johnny and Tony Randall, looking like Siamese twins. Though they were not joined at the head, Tony was one of Johnny's most frequent guests.

As a prank, Johnny once burst onto the set in the middle of a taping of Don Rickles' TV show to accuse the prickly comic of breaking his *Tonight Show* cigarette box.

Late-night personality **Jimmy Kimmel** said "Johnny made it all look easy because, for him, it was easy. He was everything the host of a television show could hope to be. Starting when I was 15 years old, I stayed up late every night to watch *The Tonight Show* on a ten-inch black and white TV set in my bedroom. The two hours of television from Johnny Carson to David Letterman were the best two hours of my day—and was probably the best two-hour block of television ever."

"His [show] was in our generation what Ed Sullivan's was to that generation. The very first time I got invited to the show, that defined [you] had now made it," said Oprah, the queen of daytime TV.

Carson chats with fellow Nebraskan Dick Cavett. They met as kids when Johnny was performing magic, and later became friends, competitors and colleagues.

Though his estranged partner Jerry Lewis was a regular guest host, Dean Martin was known to stop by for a drink as long as Johnny was serving.

On his first television appearance after his infamous free-basing accident in 1980, Richard Pryor managed to find the humor in a life-threatening experience.

Lucille Ball, at a Friar's Club roast in 1979 said there were two great guys who changed her sleeping habits: Johnny and her husband.

Carson emulating the idol of his teenage years, Jack Benny.

No, Tom, that's not a mirror. Johnny dresses up as the *Magnum PI* star during one of his many visits.

Sammy Davis Jr., who first appeared on *The Tonight Show* in 1970, came back repeatedly over the years.

Elizabeth Taylor, who had more spouses than Carson, was a good-natured guest.

Material man meets material girl during Madonna's only appearance on Carson's *Tonight Show*.

Johnny avoided doing his impression of the ex-actor when Reagan came by as a guest.

Side by Side

ED MCMAHON

"He was like a brother to me, even after retirement. . . Whenever a big career decision needed to be made, I always got the OK from the 'boss'".

The former carnival barker signed on as Carson's announcer for the 1958 quiz show *Who Do You Trust?*, kicking off a 34-year run as second banana. "Off-camera, we were pals," said McMahon in his autobiography, *For Laughing Out Loud.* "But there

The other Mod Squad: Doc, Carson, and McMahon

was always the underlying element that he was the boss. Johnny Carson was very much the same person the day we met in 1958 as when we did the last of thousands of shows together in 1992. He was direct, polite and private. . . On the air I became the big guy who drank and ate too much. I was, 'Big Ed,' who is the announcer on this show only because he never passed the bar. In fact, he never passed any bar.

"The afternoon of our first show, as we were going down to the stage, I said, "John, I want to discuss something with you. How do you see my role down here tonight?

"'Ed,' he told me, 'I don't even know how I see my own role. Let's just go down there and entertain the hell out of them.' That was the only advice I ever got from him."

"We're more effective than birth-control pills."
Johnny Carson

DOC SEVERINSEN

Doc Severinsen took over as leader of *The Tonight Show* Band in 1967 after Skitch Henderson, the original band leader, left the show. Severinsen had toured with the bands of Benny Goodman, Tommy Dorsey, and Charlie Barnet.

A generation of American men looked to Carson for the model of a well-dressed man. Johnny cashed in with his own clothing line, Johnny Carson Apparel, which at its height generated annual revenues of $75 million. Johnny himself couldn't buy off-the-rack: with a fit 32-inch waist and 41-inch shoulders, he needed all of his suits to be custom tailored. Here he and Ed are the epitome of 70s style.

Heeeeeere's Johnny!

With Johnny, an expression could be worth a thousand words.

Guest Hosts

In May 1972 Carson began offering Monday nights to a guest host: Joey Bishop, Joan Rivers, Bob Newhart, John Davidson, David Brenner, McLean Stevenson, Jerry Lewis, and David Letterman were in the chair most often. Joan Rivers became the first permanent guest host between 1983 and 1986. In 1987, Jay Leno won the permanent guest host gig.

His 177 appearances behind the desk made former Rat-Packer Joey Bishop by the far the most frequent guest host.

McLean Stevenson, who starred on the hit TV show *M*A*S*H*, took the Monday night slot fifty-eight times.

David Letterman credits Carson with giving him his big break: "He gave me a shot on his show and in doing so, he gave me a career."

"I liked him very much as a comedian and as a person" said the unlikely guest host Woody Allen (here interviewing Ursula Andress) of Carson.

"All of us who came after are pretenders. We will not see the likes of him again . . . a night doesn't go by that I don't ask myself 'What would Johnny have done?'"

David Letterman

"Johnny's really very generous. He leads me into places where I don't want to go—usually, I think just to see the expression of confusion on my face," said popular guest host Bob Newhart.

A young Jerry Seinfeld was a frequent recipient of Carson's coveted "OK" sign. Seinfeld credits his first *Tonight Show* appearance in 1981 with launching his career.

Always the fashion plate, Leno first appeared on *The Tonight Show* March 2, 1977 wearing a green suit. As Johnny put it, "This is Jay Leno's first appearance on *The Tonight Show*. Somewhere in the Midwest a scarecrow's missing his suit".

"The Carson show changed your life. If Carson liked you, you were set." The permanent guest host from 1983–1986, Joan Rivers fell from Johnny's favor when she left to host a rival talk show. The two never spoke again.

Joan Rivers gets some inspiration for her future jewelry line from David Lee Roth.

Through the Years

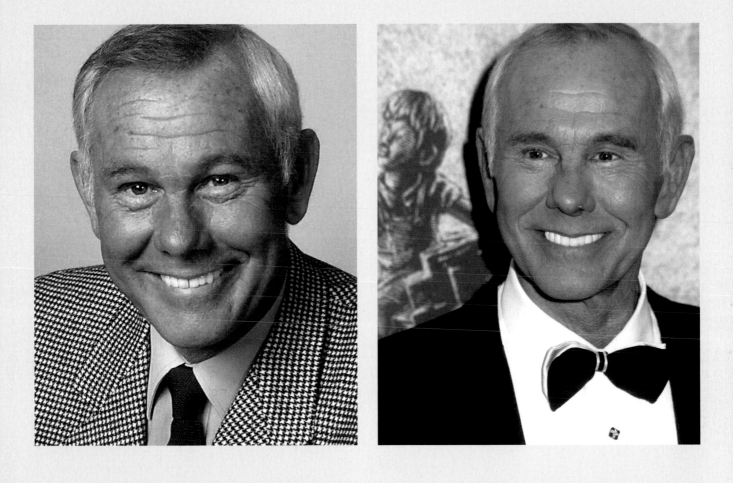

The Brouhaha:
Who Shall Inherit the Kingdom?

There was no clearly-anointed crown prince to succeed Johnny. Permanent *Tonight Show* guest host Jay Leno and star of the Carson-produced *Late Show* Dave Letterman each had a valid claim to the throne.

When NBC made the call to select Leno as the next host, believing that Dave would not be able to soften his late-night edginess for the more toned-down sensibility of the 11:30 time slot, Letterman felt the studio had betrayed him. Then CBS offered him an 11:30 slot, $12 million a year and the Ed Sullivan theater. Dave took the bait, and the late-night war between him and Jay was on.

Four giants of late night, though Gary Shandling (center, left) only played one on TV.

Dave, interviewing Jay from the seat which, ironically, one day would be his.

"I remember when [CBS president] Jim Aubrey canned Jack Benny—and I made sure that it wouldn't happen to me. I always said I'll know when the time has come."

Johnny Carson in The Club Rules
by Paul Rosenfield

The Final Episodes:
Johnny's Goodbye

Johnny's retirement in 1992 was a national event, though the show that preceded his finale on the air, which featured Bette Midler and Robin Williams as guests, was the one most of his fans remembered more than the finale itself. Midler's version of "One for My Baby (and One More for the Road)" left the audience and the host in tears.

"I was his last guest, and it was one of the most moving experiences of my life," said Bette Midler, who first performed on *The Tonight Show* in 1970.

"Anyone looking at the show 100 years from now will probably have no trouble understanding what made Carson so widely popular and what permitted him such longevity. He was affable, accessible, charming and amusing, not just a very funny comedian but the kind of guy you would gladly welcome into your home," said Tom Shales, *Washington Post* TV critic, at his 1992 retirement.

More than 22,000 guests appeared on *The Tonight Show* during Johnny Carson's thirty-year tenure as host. That's enough to fill a couch eight miles long.

JOHNNY'S FINAL MONOLOGUE

I would like to do the whole thing over again. It's been a hell of a lot of fun. As an entertainer, it has been the great experience of my life, and I cannot imagine finding something in television after I leave tonight that would give me as much joy and pleasure, and such a sense of exhilaration, as this show has given me...

My family is here tonight... And I realize that being an offspring of someone who is constantly in the public eye is not easy... So guys, I want you to know that I love you; I hope that your old man has not caused you too much discomfort. It would have been a perfect evening if their brother Rick would have been here with us, but I guess life does what it is supposed to do. And you accept it and you go on... The greatest accolade I think I received: G.E. named me "Employee of the Month." And God knows that was a dream come true.

His last time before that famous curtain.

Johnny, in one of his only on-air displays of emotion,
bids farewell to his beloved audience.

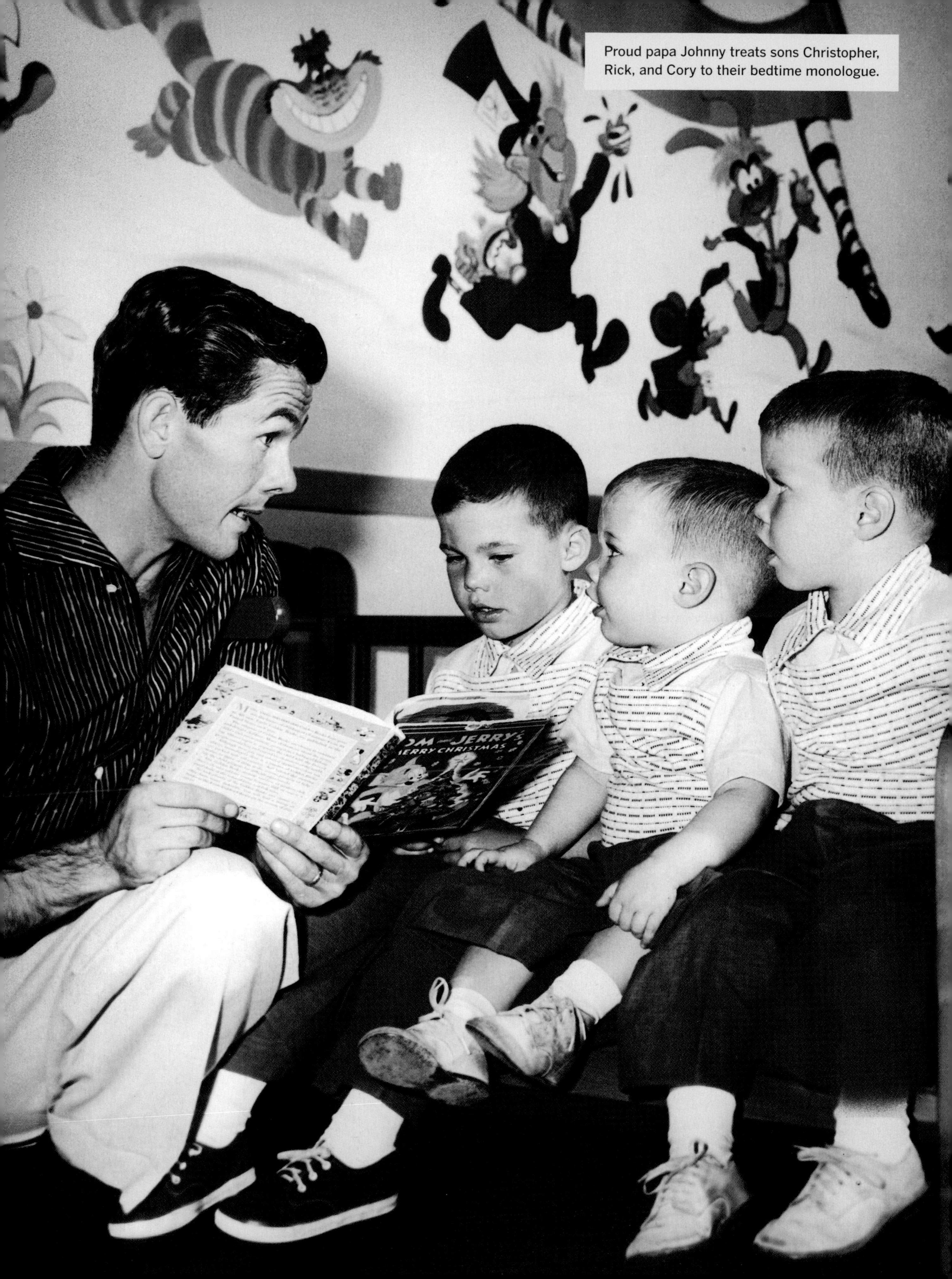

Proud papa Johnny treats sons Christopher, Rick, and Cory to their bedtime monologue.

Out of the Spotlight:
Johnny's Personal Life

cMahon noted in his 1998 autobiography that Carson was incredibly shy off camera. "He was great with 10 million people, lousy with ten." Betty Rollin wrote that off-camera he was "Testy, defensive, preoccupied, withdrawn, and wonderfully inept and uncomfortable with people." Kenneth Tynan concluded that talking to him privately was like "addressing an elaborately wired security system."

"He was not knowable, really," frequent guest and occasional host Robert Klein told the *New York Times*. "It must have been tough being married to him, but luckily that wasn't my problem." Carl Reiner agreed. "He didn't really talk to you on the commercial breaks," he said. "If you had bons mots off camera, he thought it was wasted. It wouldn't be the same the second time you told the story."

He preferred staying home to a night on the town, and favored card tricks over conversation at parties. *The Tonight Show* was always his number one priority. He'd been around long enough to know television's basic truth: ratings are everything.

"My bugging point is low. I'm not gregarious. I'm a loner. I've always been that way."

Johnny Carson

Carson's hobbies included archery and astronomy.

LOVE AND MARRIAGE

Johnny told the *Los Angeles Times* in 1986: "If I had given as much to marriage as I gave to *The Tonight Show*, I'd probably have a hell of a marriage."

Johnny was married four times: Wife number one was Jody Wolcott (1949–63), the high school sweetheart with whom he had three sons: Chris, Cory, and Rick, who died in a car accident at 39. Next came Joanne Copeland (1963–72). Third was Joanna Holland (1972–85). And he married Alexis Maas in 1987.

Johnny usually kept his personal life out of view. One exception came when the *National Enquirer* claimed his marriage was headed towards divorce. The week that issue hit the stands, Johnny unexpectedly held up a copy of the paper in the middle of the broadcast and spoke his mind.

Jody said she dyed her hair blonde after the birth of their second child in an effort to recapture Johnny's interest.

Johnny and Joanne remained friendly after their divorce. She later earned a Ph.D in nutrition and hosted her own talk show.

"I want to go on record right here in front of the American public because this is the only forum I have. They have this publication. I have this show. This is absolutely, completely, 100 percent falsehood . . . I'm going to call the *National Enquirer*, and the people who wrote this, liars. Now that's slander. They can sue me for slander. You know where I am, gentlemen."

Johnny also let down his guard to thank viewers for their expressions of sympathy after his son Rick's death. "These have not been the most happy several weeks," he said as he showed a picture of his son. "I'm not doing this to be mawkish, believe me." He asked the audience to "forgive a father's pride" and ended the broadcast with a slide show of Rick's nature photographs, the last of which was of a sunset.

Carson was in the midst of his divorce from second wife Joanne when fashion model Joanna Holland caught his eye at New York's swanky 21 club.

"If variety is the spice of life, marriage is the big can of leftover Spam."

Johnny Carson

Alexis reportedly first turned Johnny's head when she strolled by his Malibu beach house in a bikini. The statuesque blonde was formerly an aide to presidential hopeful Michael Dukakis.

First wife Jody played the magician's assistant during
The Great Carsoni's adolescent performances.

"[Johnny]
advised me to
make sure to let
my boy know
that I love him
very much, and
he kept telling
me this over
and over."

Robert Klein

Johnny's children avoided the limelight just
like their dad. "We must have inherited the
privacy gene," said Cory.

The Great Carsoni entertains a second generation with his sleight of hand.

Carson reportedly gave his grown sons an annual $35,000 Christmas check.

The first woman off the marital merry-go-round, Jody remarried in 1972.

"He was everything to me," says Joanne, pictured here at the couple's wedding reception. "He was always my protector."

Johnny and Joanne enjoyed many happy years. Unfortunately, the wedded bliss did not last.

Joanne described her ex-husband as "a little boy from the Midwest with impeccable manners."

Joanne observed, "[Johnny] wanted to bring laughter into people's lives to end their day. He was there to make people feel better. And he did."

Carson's camera-shy parents Homer and Ruth protected their personal lives even more than their famous son.

Johnny never forgot his roots. Over the years, he donated more than $4 million to institutions in Nebraska and Iowa (where he was born), including a cancer center named for his parents.

Johnny and Joanna were wed in a top-secret ceremony in 1974. He broke the news at the celebration of his tenth anniversary at *The Tonight Show*.

Carson and then-girlfriend Joanna were in crisis when she refused to leave her native New York after Johnny moved his show west. Less than a month into their bicoastal relationship, Johnny stormed back to New York and issued a proclamation: "You're coming to California," he told her, "and we're going to be married.

"The difference between divorce and a legal separation is that a legal separation gives a husband time to hide his money."

Johnny Carson

> "I know you're married to the same woman for sixty-nine years. It must be very inexpensive."
>
> *Johnny Carson*

A night out on the town with super-agent Swifty Lazar.

Carson readily admitted that his lifelong drumming hobby was an outlet for hostility.
Celebrated percussionist Buddy Rich gave Johnny his very own kit.

Angie Dickinson dated Johnny before he married Alexis, and remained friendly with him afterwards.

"As much as he loved that show and loved jokes," says *Laugh-In* producer and longtime Carson friend George Schlatter, "I think the real love of his life was Alex."

After three marriages to "J's," Carson finally made the "A" list. He and Alexis hobnobbed with NBC anchor Tom Brokaw at an NBC event.

Alexis met legends from the golden age of Broadway and the golden age of television when Johnny introduced her to Carol Channing and George Burns.

Friends reported that Carson mellowed once the show was behind him. Peter Lassally told the *Washington Post*'s Tom Shales, "He was so much sweeter and relaxed and it was so much fun to be with him."

Leisure Time

After he abdicated the late-night throne in 1992, Carson turned down almost all requests for TV appearances and interviews. Most of his retirement was spent in his sixteen-room cliffside Malibu mansion with his wife Alexis. He spent a good deal of time on his yacht, the 125-foot, cream-colored *Serengeti*, cruising the Intracoastal waterway. Closer to home, he would dine at Granita, Wolfgang Puck's Malibu restaurant, or play cards with pals Carl Reiner, Steve Martin, and Neil Simon. In 1993, he took one of two trips to East Africa (after first brushing up on his Swahili for three months). A loyal tennis fan, he also made annual trips to Wimbledon.

An investor in the DeLorean automobile company, car aficionado Carson insisted on driving himself to work every day.

"The only thing money gives you is the freedom of not worrying about money."

Johnny Carson

Although Carson was expected to make occasional appearances on NBC programs after his retirement, it never happened. In 1993, he dropped in on Bob Hope's televised ninetieth birthday special. The following year, during a Los Angeles taping of *The Late Show*, he drove up in a convertible to deliver the Top Ten list to his protégé, David Letterman. He also did the voiceover of the animated version of himself on *The Simpsons'* 1993 season finale. But he consistently refused requests for interviews: "I will not even talk to myself without an appointment," he insisted. He preferred to leave his legacy exactly as it stood.

In 1992 Carson won a Presidential Medal of Freedom. The first President Bush said, "With decency and style he's made America laugh and think."

In 1993, he received a Kennedy Center Honor for career achievement. One of the highlights of the event, which was hosted by President Bill Clinton, was David Letterman's list of the Top Ten things we miss about Carson: "Number Ten: Got laughs without cheap gimmicks like Top Ten lists." The audience of 2,700 gave Johnny no fewer than three standing ovations.

Only days before his death it was revealed that Johnny had secretly written some jokes for David Letterman. "I think the thing [Johnny] misses the most is the monologue," Carson's executive producer and longtime friend Peter Lassally said on CBS News. "When he reads the paper every morning, he can think of five jokes off the bat that he wishes he has an outlet for. He was like a little kid when Dave would do one of his jokes." And of course it was ultimate Johnny for him to keep it secret; even if he was helping Dave, he would never disrespect Leno by looking like he'd chosen sides in the late-night wars.

In a 1988 broadcast, Arkansas governor Bill Clinton reversed his flagging fortunes with "Summertime" on the sax. The two titanic personalities met again when the Kennedy Center honored Carson in 1992.

"I know full well that he missed [the show], that he. . . could never be very happy without a show to do, but part of him didn't want to admit that. He would make brave statements to the press, like, 'I'm reading' or 'I'm getting a boat,' but I think he probably hated leaving the show as much as anybody ever hated anything."

Dick Cavett

> "I know a man who gave up smoking, drinking, sex, and rich food. He was healthy right up to the day he killed himself."
>
> *Johnny Carson*

"He kidded me about my yacht," Ed McMahon told Katie Couric. "My yacht could be a dinghy on his yacht."

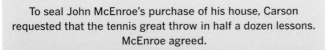

To seal John McEnroe's purchase of his house, Carson requested that the tennis great throw in half a dozen lessons. McEnroe agreed.

Beam me up, Johnny! William Shatner and Carson exchange hellos while watching a tennis match.

In September of 1996, Johnny went home to Norfolk, Nebraska for the 100th birthday of Fay Gordon, his high school English and penmanship teacher. "I'll say he was an above-average student to please him," she once jibed. "But he wasn't."

Remembering
Johnny

"Anyone who does this for a living is trying in vain to be Johnny Carson. To me, he'll always be the face, the voice, and the spirit of late-night television."
Conan O'Brien

"He never made you look bad. He wasn't like, 'Can you top this?' He always had fun with you and made you feel like you were the guy he wanted to be a hit."
Don Rickles

" He defined the original talk show, and I think there is not a person who has either watched him over the years, or certainly those of us who had the honor of experiencing him in person, who don't realize what a great loss this is."
Oprah Winfrey

"He had it all: a little bit of devil, a whole lot of angel, wit, charm, good looks, superb timing, and great, great class."
Bette Midler

"He was a giant. We're all going to miss him and I'm sure he'll always be remembered."
Regis Philbin

"Whenever I needed a trip out to California to audition for something, and I couldn't pay for it, they'd always have me on the show to pay for it. In a way he kind of sponsored my auditions so I was very grateful for that."
Susan Sarandon

"He welcomed me on his show when no one knew who I was and helped promote the image of bodybuilding . . . he brought out the best in people."
Arnold Schwarzenegger

"He'll just make a mark as probably the most unique and strongest, most powerful personality in the history of that whole box."
Jackie Mason

For her appearance on Johnny's second to last episode, Bette Midler, Marc Shaiman, and Bruce Vilanch rewrote Judy Garland's version of "You Made Me Love You" to suit the occasion.

YOU MADE ME WATCH YOU
I DIDN'T WANNA DO IT
JACK PARR HAD PUT ME THROUGH IT

YOU MADE ME WATCH YOU
I LOVE THE JOKES YOU'RE FLOGGIN'
WHEN YOU ARE MONOLOGUE-IN'

I WATCHED YOUR HAIR TURN SLOWLY
FROM DARK TO WHITE
AND WHEN I CAN'T SLEEP
I COUNT YOUR WIVES AT NIGHT

I'D DROP MY DRAWERS FOR
THE KIND OF BUCKS YOU'RE MAKING
FOR SIMPLE DOUBLE-TAKING

BEFORE YOU BID ADIEU
DON'T BE CHEAP
PUT DeCORDOVA TO SLEEP

JUST THE THOUGHT YOU'RE LEAVING
SURE GIVES ME THE SHIVERS
ARSENIO IS AT THE GATE
AND SO'S JOAN RIVERS!
YOU KNOW THEY MADE ME WATCH YOU!

HOW I'LL MISS THE SOCIAL INTERCOURSE SO VARIED
NOW I'LL HAVE TO HAVE IT
WITH THE GUY I MARRIED
YOU KNOW I'D RATHER WATCH YOU!!

Photo Credits

FRONT COVER

AP/Wideworld

The following abbreviations indicate where a photo can be found on a page: T=top, M=middle, B=bottom, L=left, R=right.

AP/WIDEWORLD

AP/Wideworld: 9, 20, 21 B, 22 T, 32, 56, 57 T, 57 B, 59, 61 L, 63 T, 64, 67 BL

Associated Press, *Norfolk Daily News*: 8 TL, 66 B, 75 BR

CORBIS

Bettmann/CORBIS: 6 T, 6 B, 7, 13 B, 18 T, 37

Jeffrey Markowitz/CORBIS SYGMA: 74

GETTY

AFP/Getty Images: 50 TR

Getty Images: 10, 11, 12, 14 TL, 14 TR, 14 B, 15, 27 T, 53 R, 58, 60 L, 60 R, 61 R, 62 T, 62 B, 63 BL, 63 BR, 65 T, 66 T, 75 BL

Time Life Pictures/Getty Images: 13 T, 69, 72 B, 78

GLOBE

Allan S. Adler/IPOL/Globe Photos, Inc.: 35 T, 40 B

Suzie Bleeden/Globe Photos, Inc.: 26 B, 27 BL, 42 T, 51 B

Nate Cutler/Globe Photos, Inc.: 45

Ralph Dominguez/Globe Photos, Inc.: 71 T

Joel Elkins/Globe Photos, Inc.: 49 B

Globe Photos, Inc.: 22 B, 30 B, 31 T, 36, 39 B, 41 T, 43 B, 48 B, 52 L, 52 R, 54, 55 T, 67 TR

NBC/Globe Photos, Inc.: 4, 8 BR, 16, 17, 18 B, 19, 21 T, 23, 25, 26 T, 27 BR, 28, 29, 30 T, 31 B, 33 T, 33 M, 33 B, 34, 35 B, 38 T, 38 B, 40 T, 40 M, 41 B, 42 B, 43 TL, 43 TR, 44, 46 L, 46 R, 47 L, 47 R, 48 T, 49 T, 50 TL, 51 T, 53 L, 72

William Regan/Globe Photos, Inc.: 75 T

Carroll Seghers/Globe Photos, Inc.: 24

WIRE IMAGE

Jonathan Alcorn/WireImage.com: 77

Betty Galella/WireImage.com: 50 B

Ron Galella/WireImage.com: 65 B, 68 T, 68 M, 73, 75 M

Jim Smeal/WireImage.com: 71 B

Leigh Weiner/WireImage.com: 39 T

Time Inc. Home Entertainment

Publisher: Richard Fraiman Executive Director, Marketing Services: Carol Pittard Director, Retail & Special Sales: Tom Mifsud

Marketing Director, Branded Businesses: Swati Rao Assistant Financial Director: Steven Sandonato Prepress Manager: Emily Rabin

Marketing Manager: Laura Adam Associate Book Production Manager: Suzanne Janso Associate Prepress Manager : Anne- Michelle Gallero

Associate Marketing Manager: Taylor Greene

Special Thanks: Varun Arora, Moira Bailey, Bozena Bannett, Alexandra Bliss, Glenn Buonocore, Bernadette Corbie, Charles Guardino, Peter Harper, Robert Marasco, Brooke McGuire, Mark Polomski, Jonathan Polsky, Celine Wojtala

Special Thanks to Imaging: Patrick Dugan, Eddie Matros

ISBN: 0-7607-7248-7

People Books is a trademark of Time Inc. We welcome your comments and suggestions about People Books. Please write to us at: People Books, Attention: Book Editors, PO Box 11016, Des Moines, IA, 50336-1016. If you would like to order any of our hardcover Collector's Edition books, please call us at 1-800-327-6388. (Monday through Friday, 7:00 a.m.- 8:00 p.m. or Saturday, 7:00 a.m.- 6:00 p.m. Central Time).

Produced by Downtown Bookworks Inc. President: Julie Merberg Executive Editor: Patty Brown Written by: David Katz and Michael Robin

Designed by: Georgia Rucker Design Photo Researcher: Sarah Parvis Production Editors: John Glenn and Sara Newberry

Special thanks to: Nanny Selma